Farming

In Britain few of the small mixed farms
that grew enough crops and raised enough
animals to supply the needs of the
local community remain. They have
mostly been replaced by larger, more
productive farming businesses.

WAYS OF LIFE

Farming

BY BRIAN WILLIAMS

Illustrated by Gwen Green

RSVP
**RAINTREE
STECK-VAUGHN**
P U B L I S H E R S
The Steck-Vaughn Company

Austin, Texas

Published by Raintree Steck-Vaughn Publishers, an imprint of Steck-Vaughn Company

Designed and produced by AS Publishing

Library of Congress Cataloging-in-Publication Data
Williams, Brian, 1943–
    Farming / by Brian Williams ; illustrated by Gwen Green.
      p.   cm. — (Ways of life)
    Includes index.
    Summary: Discusses farming methods and concerns and describes life on different kinds of farms around the world and throughout history.
    ISBN 0-8114-4786-3
    1. Agriculture — Juvenile literature.   2. Farm life — Juvenile literature. [1. Agriculture — History.   2. Farm life.]   I. Green, Gwen, ill.   II. Title.   III. Series.
    S519.W54   1993
    630 — dc20   92-29905
                                             CIP AC

Typeset by Tom Fenton Studio, Neptune, NJ
Printed in Italy by L.E.G.O. s.p.a., Vicenza
Bound in the United States by Lake Book, Melrose Park, IL

1 2 3 4 5 6 7 8 9 0 LB 98 97 96 95 94 93

Cover credits: Hutchison Library (center), Frank Lane Picture Agency

Picture credits: Australian Overseas Information Service 30, 31; Farming Information Center 7 (bottom); Finnish Tourist Board 38 (top); Frank Lane Picture Agency 26, 28 (bottom); Hutchison Library 2, 7 (top), 8, 9, 14, 28 (top), 29, 32, 33, 34 (right), 36, 37, 38 (center), 39, 40, 41, 42, 43, 44, 47.

Contents

THE KEY TO CIVILIZATION

Farming is the world's most important industry. Farmers all over the world produce more and more food every year. Yet two-thirds of the world's people are undernourished.

The first farming communities evolved about 10,000 years ago in the Middle East. There, people first learned how to plant and harvest wild wheat. It was a tremendous step forward for humanity and the key to civilization. People no longer had to wander, hunting and gathering their food. They could stay in one place and build permanent homes. In time, they learned how to domesticate and breed wild sheep and goats, and later pigs and cattle.

Farmers who grew more food than their own family could eat were able to barter the extra for other goods or produce, and this helped the development of trade. Farming communities made laws to govern themselves. They held feasts to celebrate good harvests and learned the wisdom of storing food for use in a lean season.

Opposite: The first farmers planted wild wheat and harvested the grain with simple hand tools. Everyone helped bring in the harvest.

A Chinese farm today. In much of the world, farming methods have not changed greatly for many hundreds of years.

Modern factory farming is efficient. It gives us cheaper food, but there are people who would prefer to pay a little more so that farm animals like these caged battery hens can lead more natural lives.

Leaving the land

Until about 150 years ago, most people grew at least some of their own food. Then, as countries became industrialized, more and more people left the countryside. They moved to towns to work in factories. These workers had to buy all their food. Farmers who remained in the countryside had to produce enough food to feed them, so farms had to become more productive.

Below: In Asia farmers create extra cropland by terracing hillsides. These farmers in China are planting young rice plants in a flooded field.

Farming today

During this century, more and more people have made their homes in towns. In 1919 for example, 35 out of every 100 Americans lived off the land. The United States was a nation of farm communities. Today in the United States fewer than 3 people in 100 work on a farm. Yet American farmers produce more food than ever before.

In Europe until the 1950s many farms were small. A farmer kept a few pigs, some dairy cows, chickens and ducks in the yard, and tended small fields planted with wheat and vegetables. Now those small farms have mostly been swallowed up by large farms, where huge fields are harvested by machines. Animals may be reared by intensive methods on factory farms.

In parts of Africa, Asia, and South America farming has not changed much for centuries. People try to grow enough food for their own needs. The land in many places is infertile, and there is too little, or too much, rain for crops to grow well. As a result many farming communities are desperately poor.

Farming becomes an industry

In the developed world most modern farms are businesses. They must make a profit. The profit the farmer makes depends on the cost of producing the crops or livestock and the price they will get on the market. In addition to the wages of the farm workers, the farmer has to pay for tools and machines, seeds and fertilizers, feed and shelter for the animals, pesticides, irrigation or drainage, and getting the produce to market.

Farmers also rely on many other industries. Before our food reaches the supermarket shelves, it is generally processed and packaged. It may be fresh, frozen, canned, or preserved in some other way. The price we pay for the food we eat may bear little relation to the amount the farmer was paid for it.

In harmony with nature

Farm families are the land's caretakers. They work with nature, following the rhythm of the seasons, each of which brings different tasks. Yet they are also battling with nature, trying to make a living, to make the land yield as much as it can. Fertilizers and pesticides help farmers produce more, but they also bring risks of environmental damage, causing pollution in rivers and lakes and killing off wildlife.

Farmers everywhere celebrate a good harvest. But they also know, and endure, hard times. They are at the mercy of the soil and the climate. In parts of Africa, drought and poor soil make even surviving a struggle for farmers. Crops fail, farmers abandon the land, and people perish. The famines in Africa in the 1980s reminded the world of how precious, and vulnerable, farmland is. Each year there are more hungry mouths to feed. The world population may reach 10 billion by the year 2010. To feed these billions is a challenge for all farming communities.

Bottom: Farm families like these Nigerians share routine tasks, such as grinding beans, in much the same way as their grandparents did.

9

THE BUSINESS OF FARMING

Farmers in rich countries lead very different lives from those in poor countries. Yet they share a common bond to the land and face many similar problems. Each belongs to a living, working community.

The poor peasant farmer of Asia works with a wooden plow pulled by a buffalo. Much of his work is done by hand with the aid of the family. People who grow just enough food for their own needs are called subsistence farmers. This kind of farming still is common in much of Africa, Asia, and South America.

Most modern farmers produce cash crops or livestock to send to market. They tend to specialize in one or two crops. A North American cereal farmer sells wheat. A rancher in Argentina raises cattle for beef. An Australian sheep farmer sells wool. An orange grower in Florida grows oranges to make fruit juice, and so on.

Rich or poor, farmers are at the mercy of nature. They have to cope with storms, droughts, crop diseases, insect pests, poor harvests, and gluts.

The seasons

Farmers the world over know their land. They know their weather, too, but they cannot alter it. In temperate regions, there are four seasons each year, none of them extremely hot or cold, or too wet or dry. Farms in these regions are efficient and produce large crops. They can afford the most up-to-date farming equipment. In other regions, there are only two seasons: winter and summer, and there may be extremes of temperature, drought, or excessive rain. Farmers in these areas work hard to produce small crops. They cannot afford expensive

KINDS OF FARMING

Intensive farming is used in places such as Japan and Israel where land is scarce. Farmers use fertilizers and as many workers as they need to produce the greatest yield from each piece of land.

Extensive farming is used in places where farmland is plentiful, such as the North American prairies or the steppes of Russia. The land yields less per acre than if it were farmed intensively.

CROPS

Cereals provide the world with its staple foods. Cereals are members of the grass family of plants. They include rice, wheat, corn, barley, rye, and oats.

Vegetables include an amazing variety of food plants. Potatoes are the most important. Others, such as pulses (beans and peas), cassava, sweet potatoes and yams, cabbages, and salad crops are also important, especially in countries where meat is not eaten or is very scarce.

FARMS ANIMALS

Cattle are raised for their milk and for their meat. Dairy cattle provide milk, cheese, and other dairy products. Beef cattle provide meat. Leather comes from cattle.

Mixed farming is the typical picture-book method of farming and is practiced all around the world. The farmer grows several different crops and keeps different kinds of animals. One crop may be used to feed the animals, and if one crop fails because of the weather, another may do well.

Crop rotation Farmers who grow more than one crop rarely use the same land for the same crop two years running. They switch the crops from field to field and usually leave one of four fields lying fallow. This helps the soil to recover its fertility and helps to control the pests that feed on a particular crop.

Single-crop farming is practiced increasing now that fertilizers and pesticides can produce continually good growing conditions. Wheat, potatoes, sugar, tea, and many fruits and vegetables are grown by this method. Plantations are large farms where only one crop is usually grown.

Fruit Citrus fruits, such as oranges, lemons, and grapefruit, are the most important fruit crops. Among numerous others are bananas, dates, figs, grapes, apples, pears, peaches, plums, and strawberries.

Nuts Peanuts are an important protein crop. Others include almonds, walnuts, chestnuts, and Brazil nuts.

Oilseeds are used for making cooking oils and for processing into animal feed (and industrial products). The most important are soybeans, peanuts, cottonseeds, sunflower seeds, rapeseeds, sesame seeds, palm nuts, and olives.

Coffee, tea, and cocoa provide us with stimulating hot drinks. The leaves of the tea plant and the beans (fruit) of the other two are used.

Sugar comes from two crops: sugar-cane and sugar beets.

Fiber crops provide us with natural fabrics for clothes and other purposes. They include cotton, flax, sisal, jute, and hemp.

Rubber comes from latex, a white liquid that oozes from rubber trees when the bark is cut.

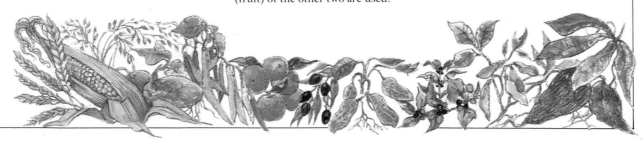

Sheep and goats Sheep are raised mostly for their wool and meat, though, like goats, they also provide milk and cheese.

Pigs are farmed intensively for their meat, which we see as pork, bacon, and ham.

Poultry are farmed for their meat and for their eggs. Besides chickens and turkeys, ducks and geese are raised on farms.

modern equipment, fertilizers, or pesticides.

Rice farmers in India and Bangladesh work through two seasons. In summer, winds from the Indian Ocean bring heavy rainfall. This is the monsoon. In winter, the winds shift direction and blow from the land to the sea, bringing dry weather. The farmers must plant their rice before the monsoon, for the torrential rains are needed to make the young plants grow.

Pestilence and drought

In northern Africa on the edge of the Sahara rains come rarely and sometimes fail altogether. Seedlings wither and die in the hot sun, so there is no harvest. There is no grazing for cattle, so they die, too. More and more land turns to desert. In desperation people move farther south, but many still die from starvation.

Even when there is enough rain for seeds to germinate, the farmers cannot count on a harvest. When crops grow well, so do pests. Swarms of locusts descend on the growing crops and strip them bare of every leaf. Aid programs concentrate on spraying the locusts at the "hopper" stage when they are too young to fly. Once they are airborne there is little chance of eradicating them.

Going to market

Getting produce from farm to table requires many operations, involving wholesalers, food processing companies, and retailers. Farmers presell their produce to customers or take it to market to sell to the highest bidder. Today perishable goods can be refrigerated, but getting fresh food to customers was a problem in the past and in many places still is. Food crops are left to rot in the fields in parts of Russia because there is no way of getting them to hungry people elsewhere in the country.

Market day

Since ancient times people have met at markets to buy and sell goods, to exchange news and gossip, and to discuss the latest prices. On a set day each week or month, farmers bring fresh fruits and vegetables, flowers, and other produce to the marketplace. If the harvest of a particular crop has been poor, prices will be high. If a crop has grown well, growers may find it hard to sell at any price—and the food may go to waste.

THE FARMER'S YEAR

Spring
Farmers plow, fertilize, and plant their fields, often working through the night by floodlight. Livestock farmers take care of newborn animals.

HARVEST TIME

In the past, whole communities went into the fields to gather the ripe crop. Harvesting grain was hard work in the days when wheat and other crops had to be cut by hand. Men, women, and children worked all day long.

Celebration
A good harvest meant there was no fear of going hungry when winter came. When the last corn was gathered, farmers, workers, and neighbors would celebrate with a thanksgiving service in church and a party.

Harvest time was generally a time of celebration in a European village in the Middle Ages. A good harvest meant food for all. A poor harvest meant a long, hungry winter for the villagers.

Summer

Summer is the growing season for crops and weeds—and the eating season for pests. Farmers use weed killers and pesticides, taking care not to harm the soil, plants, or farm animals. The animals graze and grow fat, and the crops ripen.

Autumn

Harvest time is the busiest season of the year, when traditionally everyone helps to gather in crops before bad weather spoils them. Cattle are sent to market. Pigs are sent later in the year.

Winter

Animals are fed on hay gathered earlier in the year and brought into sheds in bad weather. Farm equipment is serviced, repaired, or replaced. Farmers catch up on the paperwork and plan for the following year.

Harvest festival

People take gifts of food to church for special harvest services. Even town churches hold harvest festivals. Children help decorate the church with sheaves of corn and displays of food. People make small figures called corn dollies from wheat straw. Once these had a magical significance, but today they are mostly sold to tourists.

Harvest suppers

Harvest suppers are still held in many country districts. Everyone enjoys a hearty meal to celebrate the bounty of the harvest.

Thanksgiving

Americans celebrate Thanksgiving Day in memory of the first successful harvest gathered by the Pilgrims in the autumn of 1621. The first settlers in Massachusetts would have starved without the help of friendly Indians, who taught them how to plant beans and corn.

Corn goddess

In Europe people believed that it was bad luck to be seen by the corn goddess, whose home was the cornfields. So they cut the last few stalks very carefully, covering their faces so that the corn goddess could not recognize them.

Corn dollies

Harvest moon

The harvest moon is the full moon seen at the time of the autumnal equinox, around September 23 in the northern hemisphere. For several nights, the moon shines so brightly that farmers in northern Europe and Canada can work late into the night to bring in the harvest. In Australia the harvest moon shines during March.

Rice harvest

In Asia people celebrate the rice harvests. They bake special rice and coconut cakes to eat.

Sugarcane harvest

In Jamaica sugarcane cutters celebrate the cutting of the ripe sugarcane.

Pineapple harvest

In the Amazon region of South America, Amerindians celebrate the harvest of pineapples, cassava, and other crops.

Farmers bring horses, cattle, sheep, and pigs to town and sell them at auctions. They also come to buy, casting a critical eye over each animal as it is led around the sale ring. The auctioneer conducts the selling so fast that outsiders cannot follow what is going on, but the regulars make themselves understood with nods and gestures. Grain and other products are also auctioned.

Above: This farmer grows only bananas. Some countries, like Grenada in the Caribbean, rely on one or two cash crops, such as bananas. A banana company buys the whole crop.

Above right: Prize bull and proud handler. Agricultural shows and fairs are fun for farmers and for the public who come from the town for a taste of country living.

Many small towns still have livestock and produce markets. In Africa, Asia, and South America farmers and their families sell their produce on the street. They spread out their fruit, eggs, herbs, and other goods for passersby to inspect. Haggling (bargaining) over the price is enjoyed by buyer and seller.

Going to the fair

Most counties hold an annual fair either on a permanent or temporary fairground. This is an opportunity for everyone to show off. Farmers bring the best of their animals to be judged in competitions for each breed. Samples of fruit and vegetables and other crops are laid out to be judged by experts and admired by all.

There are horse races and horse shows, and other competitive sporting events for children. There are roller coasters, Ferris wheels, merry-go-rounds, and shooting galleries. There are fast-food stands selling hamburgers, pizzas, popcorn, ice cream, and cotton candy. All through the day bands play, and the local police force or fire brigade puts on displays.

THRILLS AND SKILLS

Farming communities enjoy entertainments that allow people to show off their skills.

Barbecues
Eating food cooked on an open fire outdoors was normal for people the world over until modern times. Barbecues are still popular with ranch and other farming peoples.

Barn dances
These "square dances" with a host to call out the sequence of moves for the dancers to make were traditional get-togethers eagerly awaited by the farm communities of the 1800s. They gave people a chance to dress up, to meet neighbors they might not have seen for months, and to make new friends. Country music and country dances are still popular today.

Rodeo
The rodeo gives everyone a chance to admire the riding skills of broncobusters and steer ropers. At a rodeo, riders try to ride bulls and unbroken horses for fun, and there are wagon races.

Sheepdog trials
In some European countries dogs are trained to look after flocks of sheep. In a sheepdog trial shepherds and their dogs compete in driving sheep around a test course. The dog responds to the whistles and calls of its master. Together they make a team.

Plowing for prizes
Farmers from about 30 countries attend a plowing competition held in Ireland each year. Competitors are judged on at least 20 aspects of the job.

Horses for pleasure
Although working horses are not seen often on farms today, many farm people enjoy horseback riding. Horse shows and races are popular all over the world. In some communities people still dress up to hunt foxes with horns and hounds.

FARMERS OF LONG AGO

Farming allowed people to stay in one place and build a settled community. Finding food no longer took up all of the people's time. They were able to develop skills in metalworking and pottery, to make new tools, and to build homes for themselves and temples to their gods.

Egypt is a hot, dry country. Through it runs the Nile River. Every year, in ancient times, the river would flood. For three months, the valley was inundated with water.

As soon as the flood was over, the farmers would plow their fields and sow their seeds. Before the next flood, there would be time to harvest three plantings. To extend the amount of farmland, the Egyptians irrigated their fields. They dug ditches from the river and filled them with water by means of a shadoof, a lever system.

Teams of long-horned oxen pulled the plows and afterward helped to trample the seeds, which were sown by hand. Crops included wheat and barley for making bread, vegetables and fruit, and flax for making clothes. Beer was made from barley, and wine from grapes.

In addition to crops, the Egyptians raised cattle, pigs, sheep, goats, ducks, geese, and other water birds. There was not much grazing land, so the animals were often fed and fattened in their stalls.

Slaves and women

The men who tended the animals and the fields were members of the family, workers paid in kind, or slaves owned by the farmer. The women stayed at home to look after the home and children, to work at weaving, and to grind the corn to make flour. They had equal status with their husbands, and many owned property.

Farmers took their surplus food to market, bartering it for goods of similar value—they did not use money.

Irrigation in ancient Egypt

Rice planting in ancient China

Shepherds in ancient Greece

Egypt was a highly organized society with virtually every aspect of life controlled by the pharaoh (the ruler) and his officials. They kept records of the amount of food a farmer produced, and they collected taxes. Each farmer had to give a proportion of his produce to fund the army and the priesthood.

Feeding China's thousands

Even in ancient times China had a teeming population with not much good farmland. The peasants made use of every bit of land. They terraced hillsides, irrigated dry areas, and built huge earthworks to prevent floods. They grew wheat, millet, corn, and soybeans in the north and rice in the south. Unable to keep up with demand for their crops from the nobles and warlords, the peasants often went hungry themselves. Just as the emperor had total power over the country, a father had total power over his family. Women worked but had little say in the running of their homes.

Working women of Greece

The Greeks were skilled farmers. Very little of their rocky land was suitable for growing crops, but they grew barley and wheat. There was little pasture, but they raised sheep and goats. Grapes and olives grew well. Their tools were mostly made of wood, and they used oxen, and in some places horses, to work their farms. The men of the family worked on the farm, the women in the home and on the farm. Poor women were more independent than rich women, who had slaves to do their work. Women might take the farm produce to market and sell it in their own stalls.

Farmers — the might of Rome

A vineyard in ancient Rome

One of the greatest empires the world has ever known originated from a small farming community. Roman farmers grew grapes and olives and other Mediterranean crops on small farms. They used iron plows yoked to oxen. They became soldiers of Rome only when the demands of their farms allowed. As Rome prospered, other men became professional soldiers.

Wealthy citizens bought up the small farms to make huge estates that employed hundreds of slaves. They rotated their crops and even understood that planting legumes periodically would make their soil more fertile.

THE MIDDLE AGES

For farmers in Europe during the Middle Ages, life was hard. Most were serfs, peasants who owned no land of their own but were obliged to rent fields from a rich landowner. They worked the noble's fields as well as their own and had few rights. They grew cereals and vegetables and kept a few pigs and cattle. Fields were usually divided into strips. Everyone had a share in areas of common land, where cattle could be grazed. One in two or one in three fields was left to lie fallow. From the little they produced in their own fields, the serfs had to pay to have their grain milled and their bread baked. They also had to make needed repairs to the estate.

A hard life

The peasants' own homes were small huts with sacks of straw for beds and maybe a yard for a few chickens. People ate mostly bread and vegetables, with eggs and chicken occasionally, and any wild creatures such as rabbits and hares that they could catch. Only the nobility could afford much meat, which could be preserved by salting or smoking. Hunting big game was reserved for the rich. In England a poor man could be hanged for killing a nobleman's deer.

Working through the seasons

Winter was the hardest time of all. Fresh food of any kind was scarce, and people often went hungry. In spring the whole community went to work in the fields. Men walked behind wooden plows pulled by oxen. Women scattered the seeds, and children acted as scarecrows to frighten away hungry birds. Children worked as hard as adults. They herded geese to market and drove pigs into the woods to root for acorns.

Harvest was a busy time for everyone. People prayed for good weather. After the rains that made the crops grow, they needed sunshine to ripen them. Come harvest time, people worked from sunrise to sunset. Grain was taken to the mill to be made into flour. Apples and nuts were picked and stored for winter. Pigs were killed, and their meat was made into bacon and ham, ready to be hung from roof beams next to bags of dried beans and peas.

Isolation and strife

Farmers in the Middle Ages worked hard to survive, but often whole villages were wiped out by disease or starvation, or by wars fought heedlessly over land. Farm communities were often isolated because roads were few and bad. People in one village often treated people in the next village, over the hill, as strangers. For them, it was an adventure to journey to town on market day to sell a cow and buy some trinkets or woolen cloth.

Medieval peasants worked on strips of land owned by a rich lord. They shared the common land, where they could graze cattle and pigs.

FARMERS OF THE AMERICAS

When Europeans first arrived in North and South America, they found that the land was farmed. The Native Americans of northeastern North America had cultivated a variety of wild plants for thousands of years. They grew corn, beans, squash, and many other vegetables. They taught the settlers how to grow and cook many foods that were strange to them.

Pioneer families in America had to be practically self-sufficient. Here the father is making bullets, the mother is making candles, and the sons and neighbors are tending crops. To survive in the New World, the newcomers had to stick together and help each other.

THE INCAS

When the Spanish arrived in South America in 1532, they found an empire in the Andes that relied on expert farming methods. The army that had carved out the empire had been well fed from storehouses filled by the work of peasant farmers, who grew mostly corn and potatoes and herded llamas. Only the river valleys were flat and fertile; the rest of the land was mountainous or desert. The farmers skillfully terraced the hillsides and irrigated the fields with canals.

The Incas were rulers of this empire. They owned all the land and dictated how it should be farmed and its produce shared. One-third of the land fed the priests and provided offerings to the gods. Another third filled the emperor's storehouses. From these, food was dispensed to soldiers, nobles, officials, and craftsmen, and to those who could not provide for themselves—widows and orphans, the old, the sick, and the disabled. The rest of the land went to the peasants. They had to work the land of the gods and the emperor before they tended their own fields.

Llamas provided the Incas with milk, meat, wool, and portage.

Clearing the land

Before they could farm their land, the settlers had to clear it. Parties of pioneers set out to make new homes in what was to them a strange and frightening wilderness. When they arrived at a good place, the first task for everyone was to rid the area of trees and rocks. They worked with axes and any tools they had brought with them. If they were lucky, established neighbors would lend them a hand. While they cleared the land, they lived in makeshift shelters with an open fire to warm them and keep wild beasts away.

Until they harvested their first crop, there would be no fresh food to eat other than animals they could catch in the forest or fish from the streams. Once they had sown their seeds, the pioneers turned their attention to building homes and furnishing them. In most areas there was no shortage of wood or craftsmen skilled in woodworking. Families worked together to raise the timbers.

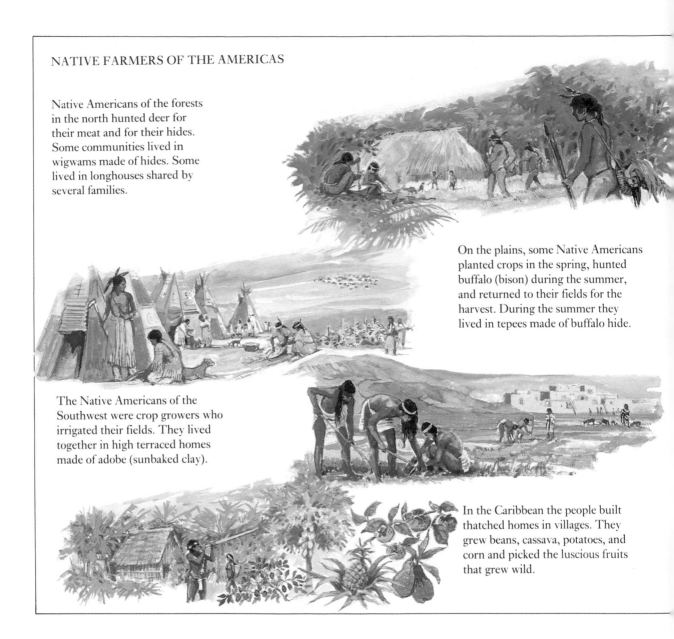

NATIVE FARMERS OF THE AMERICAS

Native Americans of the forests in the north hunted deer for their meat and for their hides. Some communities lived in wigwams made of hides. Some lived in longhouses shared by several families.

On the plains, some Native Americans planted crops in the spring, hunted buffalo (bison) during the summer, and returned to their fields for the harvest. During the summer they lived in tepees made of buffalo hide.

The Native Americans of the Southwest were crop growers who irrigated their fields. They lived together in high terraced homes made of adobe (sunbaked clay).

In the Caribbean the people built thatched homes in villages. They grew beans, cassava, potatoes, and corn and picked the luscious fruits that grew wild.

Days of toil

Once settled, the pioneers still had to battle to keep the wilderness at bay and protect themselves from hostile Native Americans whose land they had taken. The settlers built stockades around their villages, and nobody ventured out without a rifle at the ready.

Men, women, and children shared all the farm work and all the housework. There was plenty of it. There were few stores to buy goods in, so almost everything had to be homemade. Women would make cheese one day, clothes the next, and candles the following. Children would grind corn in the morning, and if they were lucky, have lessons in the afternoons. The days were rarely long enough to get all the jobs done.

Slaves from Africa

Cotton, tobacco, sugarcane, and other crops were grown on plantations in North America and the West Indies. Most of the plantations were established by British settlers. The workers on the plantations were slaves brought from Africa starting in the 1640s. The produce was generally shipped back to Europe. Until the mid-1800s slaves could be bought and sold by their white masters. Some owners treated their slaves fairly, but most slaves were forced to work long hours in gangs and received just enough food to maintain their strength. Others were treated even more cruelly. The slaves preserved memories of their African homeland in music and stories, and these have become part of African American culture in America today.

In the forests of South America, the Amerindians cleared patches of land on which to grow cassava, potatoes, peppers, corn, and manioc—a root vegetable like cassava. They lived in open-sided houses with a roof thatched with palm leaves. In some places the villagers built one big house for everyone.

The longhorn cattle of the West were wily, wild animals. Rounding them up was a lot more dangerous than driving a herd of docile modern cattle.

HOME ON THE RANGE

Cattle were brought to the New World by the Spanish in the 1500s. By the mid-1800s ranchers in the Southwest were raising cattle on the open range—vast stretches of unfenced land. Cowboys were hired to brand the animals, round them up, and drive them across the range. They lived in the saddle by day and camped by a fire at night. It was a hard, dangerous, and comfortless life.

Later ranches were fenced in. Cowboys lived together in bunkhouses, but their lives grew no less dangerous. They still had to cope with often cruel weather, cattle stampedes, and disputes with neighbors. At night the cowboys sang songs and told stories, or rode into town. There was not much time or opportunity for family life.

A tranquil country scene.
This is how townsfolk like to
imagine the countryside:
peaceful, traditional, and
unchanging. Many farms are
now large businesses, but
there are still plenty of small
family-run farms that raise
cows, pigs, poultry, and
perhaps sheep, as well as
growing root, grain, and
other crops.

TOWARD TODAY

In the 1500s richer farmers in Europe began to
"enclose" their fields. They bought land from neighbors and hedged or fenced it to keep out other
farmers' animals. This change made farms more efficient, but it affected the life of the farm community.
Many poor people once again became farm laborers,
working for a rich farmer. They no longer owned their
own plots of land. Often they lived in small houses
owned by the farmer and were unable to move away.
Some farmhands in Europe still live in tied cottages, homes
that go with the job.

Improvements in farming methods continued. New
tools and machines were invented, and new industries
established to process, package, and market food. The
farmer's wife no longer had to make cheese; it could
be done by machine. Cattle were slaughtered and their
meat packed far from the farms where they were reared.

Traditional farms disappear

By the 1900s, farms had changed even more. Some
farms were now very large. Others were run by tenants,
renting the land from a landowner. Some farms were
run by farm managers employed by agricultural companies. Machines took over much of the farm work that
had formerly been done by people. Combine harvesters
replaced gangs of workers with scythes and sickles.
Electric milking machines replaced milkmaids, and
tractors replaced horses. Traditional mixed farms were
becoming rarer, although some still exist today.

FARMING TODAY

In temperate lands where soils are fertile and there is plenty of rain, relatively few people work in farming. Traditional mixed farms that once provided a balanced diet for the local community have given way to specialized farms whose produce may be sold to people thousands of miles away. Large areas of farmland have no farm animals, and large areas no crops. In poor countries, more people work on the land but produce less than farmers in rich countries.

Large areas of the world are too cold, too dry, too mountainous, or too built up for agricultural production. These areas produce little as a result. Third World yields could be improved, however, if the countries could afford more modern farming methods.

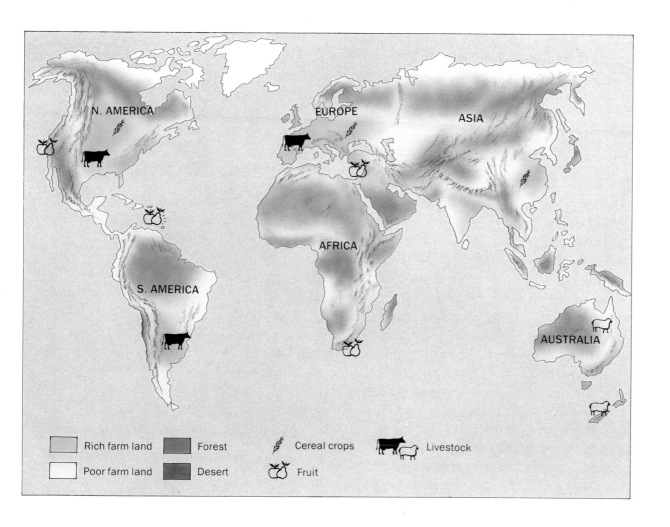

Rich farm land	Forest	Cereal crops
Poor farm land	Desert	Fruit
		Livestock

PRAIRIE GRAIN GROWERS

On the vast treeless prairies of the United States and Canada, farmers grow millions of tons of grain each year. Much is exported to countries that cannot feed their own people.

The farmers live in small and often lonely communities. From the air, the prairies look like a vast sea of wheat with clusters of farm buildings scattered here and there like islands. These enormous farms need surprisingly few people to work them because most of the work has been mechanized. Tractors haul the plows and seed drills, and at harvest time armies of combine harvesters march across the fields. The grain is stored in tall elevators that are often the only landmarks.

The North American prairies are a sea of wheat. Farmers use fertilizers to improve the soil, herbicides to control weeds, pesticides to prevent disease, and more machines than people to plow, plant, and gather the grain.

NEW WHEAT

Living in the prairie communities are many people whose ancestors were pioneer settlers. The Mennonites, for example, were a religious group who came to the United States from Russia in the 1870s. They introduced a variety of wheat, called Turkey Red, which grew well on the dry plains. This new wheat made possible the great expansion of wheat farming, especially in Kansas and other states.

New strains of wheat that will ripen quickly have produced increased yields all over the world. In places where the hours of daylight were too few to ripen old varieties, the new varieties grow with vigor.

From village to town

As farms have grown larger and transportation has become easier, traditional farming communities have virtually disappeared. The village community has become a town community. There is no need for little local stores when people can buy all they need in a shopping mall and store a year's supply of food in the freezer. There is no need for a village school when children can take the bus to town. In many villages public transportation is becoming just a memory, leaving the old and poor isolated.

The town supplies all the community's needs. It has churches and schools, doctors, hospitals and vets, shops and car showrooms, banks, and all kinds of businesses. Farmers can buy new machinery and equipment and sell their produce at the auction barns and grain elevators.

Farmers no longer call on their neighbors for help with the harvest. They hire workers and pay them the going rate for the job. They no longer rely on the Saturday night barn dance for their entertainment. They can go to restaurants and clubs or stay at home and watch television.

Keeping up with each other

In most county towns government farm agencies are available to help and advise farmers. Research into crops and farming methods brings constant improvements, so farmers make sure that they are up to date on the latest techniques and products. Although farmers compete with each other, they keep in contact, discuss problems, and pass on information to each other.

HOME ON THE RANGE

In Australia, the United States, and South America farmers raise cattle and sheep in huge numbers on enormous open ranges of grassland. These people are used to taking care of themselves, for the nearest neighbor may be miles away. Some ranches are so big that the farmers use helicopters to get around.

Modern cowboys

Once cowboys spent almost the whole working day in the saddle. Horses are still used on many ranches, but modern cowboys mostly use motorbikes or trucks. They use radios to keep in touch with the ranch boss, with their fellow workers, and with their homes.

Ranching is big business today. Huge herds of finely bred cattle are raised on lush pastures to ensure that the consumers get only the most succulent, tender beef in their hamburgers and steaks. The cattle are fed and housed in dry sheds when the weather is bad.

Though the cattle are more docile than the longhorns of old, dealing with so many animals demands strength and courage. A cowboy no longer needs a gun to fight off hostile Indians or cattle rustlers, but the modern cowboy still faces dangers. Snow in winter can bury cattle. Drought in summer parches the land, dries up water holes, and withers pasture. Storms can turn gentle streams into tumbling torrents. But life at home is a lot more comfortable.

Family life

Ranch families have cars, televisions, freezers, and other modern conveniences, and they are no longer isolated. They can drive into town to shop and visit friends. Children take the bus to school. They eat the same fast food and watch the same television shows as everyone else. Though most ranch children learn to ride and occasionally see a visiting rodeo show, rodeo riders on bucking broncos are more familiar to them in movies than in real life.

Above: The gauchos are the cowboys of South America. Riding across the pampas, or grasslands, they herd the beef cattle for which Argentina is famous.

Opposite: Cattle are pampered to produce fine beef. They eat ten times more food than they produce. In less developed countries meat is a luxury few people can afford.

Right: The busy stockyards of Oklahoma handle millions of cattle raised on the ranches of this beef-producing state.

The heart of Australia is desert. Vast sheep stations in the outback produce enough pasture for sheep on land that would be too dry to grow crops. Motorcycles are often used to round up the sheep.

FARMERS "DOWN UNDER"

Many farms in Australia and New Zealand remain family businesses in which family members share the work. A dairy farm in New Zealand, for example, might have 130 cows. Only two people are needed to take care of the cattle, so a father and one son usually manage it. Instead of riding horses or walking, they ride around on motorbikes. The father's other children must find work in town.

Milk from cows is made into dairy foods such as butter and cheese. Often farmers organize cooperatives to make and sell these dairy foods.

Faraway farmers

Farming can be a lonely life. Farmers may spend a day on the farm without seeing anyone. So they look forward to the next trip to town for a chat with neighbors about farm prices and to catch up with the local news. Dairy farmers know that if they go to bed late, they still have to

Teams of sheepshearers travel from station to station. With so many millions of sheep to be sheared, the shearers take pride in the speed with which they can cut away the fleeces without harming the sheep.

The doctor comes by air in isolated parts of Australia.

Education comes over the air for these Australian children who live hundreds of miles from the nearest school.

be up early for the morning milking. Children have to be up early, too, to make the long bus journey to school. Their mothers may only get to town every few months. Many farms are so isolated that people have to travel to town by plane.

Many children receive their education without ever moving from their homes. They do their lessons by radio. When people are sick, the doctor may fly in to visit them. If they are very ill, they are airlifted to a hospital.

Alone with hundreds of sheep

The loneliest life is that of the hill shepherd. He or she has a dog and a flock of sheep for company. In Australia huge flocks of sheep are kept on ranches called sheep stations. Once a year, at shearing time, a contractor's shearing gang arrives. The shearers go from station to station, working at great speed. They are proud of their skill and take part in hotly contested competitions to see who is the fastest and best shearer.

SURVIVING IN ASIA

Farmers in rich countries often complain. They complain about high taxes and low prices; about the expense of buying new tractors, fuel for heating, fertilizers, and animal feed. A poor peasant farmer in an overcrowded country like Bangladesh in Asia faces even more serious problems.

Bangladesh is a flat land with many rivers. It is a desperately poor country with few natural resources. Yet it is home to more than 104 million people. Farmers in Bangladesh struggle to grow food for themselves. Their greatest enemy is flooding because the land is so low-lying and open to the sea. Farmers plant their crops on fields raised on mud banks for protection against floodwaters.

Few farmers in Bangladesh have money to buy tractors or fertilizers. The people build their own houses. Women work as hard as men, helping to till the

This Indian woman has to carry home huge bundles of leaves to burn as fuel for cooking the family meal.

Bangladeshi farmers in a rice field. Bangladesh is very flat and low-lying. Mud banks offer little protection to crops or homes when cyclones, or hurricanes, strike, and terrible floods occur.

soil with wooden hand plows. There is endless work and almost no leisure.

Families at work

In Europe and America there are now fewer family farms. But family farming is still common in Asia. In India the oldest man in the family owns the land. Three or four generations share a home. Young men do not move away when they marry. When a woman marries, she goes to live with her husband's family. She brings an extra pair of hands to help with the work but also an extra mouth to feed.

On a peasant farm in Asia or Africa women often do the heavy work. They carry water from the well, fertilize the fields with cattle dung, and gather firewood for cooking. In semidesert lands, where trees are scarce, collecting firewood may take hours every day. Some farmers burn cow dung on their cooking fires and so waste a valuable natural fertilizer.

CYCLONE PERIL

From time to time, terrible tropical storms called cyclones rush in from the Bay of Bengal. The winds drive the sea inland. Water pours over the farmers' fields, villages are swamped, houses are swept away, and cattle drowned. Many people lose their few precious possessions. Sometimes thousands of people die.

Despite these natural disasters, the farmers of Bangladesh do not give up. Each new season brings renewed hope. Even after a cyclone, people return to their land as soon as the waters have fallen. They rebuild their homes, plow the salt-soaked soil, and plant new seeds for a new harvest. Aid from richer countries is some help, but the villagers themselves must do most of the manual labor to reclaim the drowned land.

PLANTATIONS

The tea in your tea bag may have come from the leaves of a bush growing on a hillside in India or Sri Lanka. Women pick the leaves from the plants by hand and drop them into baskets hung on their backs. The leaves are taken to the tea estate factory, where other workers watch over the rolling machines, fermentation tables, and driers that turn the fresh green leaves into dark fragments ready for packing.

Most plantations are owned by large international companies. They are factory farms, employing large numbers of workers. Much of the work, picking the leaves from tea bushes for example, is done by women. They work hard, often for low wages.

Some plantation workers live in houses built by the company. Often in the past such workers were not much better off than slaves. Because they were forced to buy goods from company-owned stores, workers often got into debt. They ended up working just to repay the company that employed them.

PEASANT FARMERS OF THE ANDES

In the high Andes Mountains of South America, peasant farmers till the soil much as their ancestors did hundreds of years ago. Some farmers still use digging sticks instead of spades and oxen instead of tractors. It is bitterly cold in the thin air of the bleak highlands, and few crops grow well. Often the people go hungry.

Wage slaves

In the past the Indians of the Andes were treated as slaves by the Spanish conquerors. Today they have regained some of their lost lands, though most of the best land is owned by wealthy families. The landowners employ workers for low wages to plant and harvest profitable crops. Where government land reforms have given land back to the people, they still have problems. Many people are too poor to buy seeds, let alone fertilizers or the machines and equipment they need to irrigate and run their farms.

Farming in Peru, in the
foothills of the Andes
Mountains. Oxen are used
to plow the valley soil, but
there is much backbreaking
work for the peasants, often
with little reward.

Others manage to produce enough to feed the family
and travel to the market in town to sell potatoes, beans,
corn, and herbs. They accept cash, instead of bartering
goods as they once did. Some can afford to buy a radio or
television, or even a secondhand motorbike or truck.
Some young people do not stay in the mountain villages but drift to the towns and cities, looking for
jobs. They often wind up jobless and homeless, living in
squalid shantytowns. Many resort to crime.

SUBSISTENCE IN AFRICA

In West Africa a farm family hopes to grow all the vegetables it needs. The people plant yams, corn, cassava, okra, and peppers, as well as bananas and oil palm trees. Children go to school on weekdays, often walking a long distance through the forest to get there. On weekends they help their parents. The busiest time is the rainy season, from March to September, when weeds spring up all over the vegetable plots. Then everyone goes to work with hoes and machetes (long broad-bladed knives).

The children may enjoy their work on the farm, but many see their future in the city. There they may have an opportunity to go to college and study for careers in medicine, law, and business. Others may work in

Right: This farmer in Ghana has a fine crop of yams. They are probably his only crop, which he will sell to feed his family and buy other goods.

Below: A Masai cattle herder. These East African people are nomads, moving with their herds to find fresh grazing.

Above: In Africa women often look after the children and the family vegetable plot, while the men are away hunting, tilling the fields, or these days, finding work in mines or factories.

factories or drive a truck for a living. As more young people drift away, villages die. Only older people remain, and they cannot keep the land cultivated.

Old ways die

When the old system of subsistence farming breaks down, families can no longer grow enough food to feed themselves. The government has to buy food from abroad. This imported food must be paid for from cash crops grown on large plantations where workers are paid wages for their labor. Governments in parts of Africa have concentrated on new factories and big plantations where they use modern farming methods and equipment. They have neglected the small farmers, who once grew all the food the people needed.

CATTLE HERDERS OF AFRICA

In parts of Africa people look upon cattle as wealth. A farmer with many cows is rich, no matter how little milk or meat they provide. The Masai people of East Africa are famous as cattle herders and lion hunters. The cattle are herded into the village at night, protected by a thornbush fence from attack by hungry lions. A traditional Masai village house is made of mud and dried cow dung. Women live in one room, men in another. The remaining room is shared by children and calves.

The seasonal cycle

Village farmers move to and from their fields as the seasons change. In Botswana, in southern Africa, people leave their villages to plant the seeds in the fields in spring after the rainy season. School ends so that older children can help. Only old people and little children are left at home.

Boys help to drive the cattle out to graze on the new grass. As the crops ripen in the hot season, streams run dry, and the grass withers. Then the cattle must be brought back to the village, where they can be given drinking water from the well. The villagers return to the fields to bring in the harvest of grain. Village life resumes until the rains come again. People spend the rainy season at home, getting their tools ready for the next planting.

NOMADIC HERDERS

Nomads are people who have no fixed homes but wander with their herds to find fresh grass for their animals to eat. Some nomads keep camels or goats, others drive flocks of sheep. Their animals provide them with milk, meat, and clothing.

Living on the steppes

The herding peoples of eastern Russia and Mongolia are expert horseback riders. Their traditional homes are tents, called yurts, made from animal skins. Small boys are given the job of looking after the cattle and sheep. But

the horses are half-wild, and it takes experienced riders to round them up. The animals are vital to the nomads' lives. A nomad family will often bring lambs and goat kids into their tent at night for the warmth they provide.

On the vast treeless steppes of Central Asia a family may travel 60 miles to visit relatives. Normally members of the family meet only in the evening for the

Opposite: Today, though few Lapps still wander with their reindeer, they keep up traditional appearances. Their brightly colored clothes contrast sharply with the bleakness of their land.

Right: The Bedouin of North Africa and the Middle East are desert people. Camel herders are aristocrats. Lower on the social scale are sheep and goat herders.

main meal of the day. During the day, the men and boys make do with a snack of cheese soaked in tea. The tea is made from Chinese tea bricks brewed in water with salt, flour, butter, and milk.

Change comes to the nomads

The Lapp people of Scandinavia live north of the Arctic Circle. Here the sun does not shine for two months of the year, and winter lasts for nine months. It is so bitterly cold that few plants grow. Until valuable metals were found there, the snow-covered land provided only one resource—reindeer.

For many centuries the Lapps roamed with their reindeer herds, dependent on the animals for all their needs, including transportation. It was impossible for them to settle in one place because the vegetation was so sparse. They built huts of turf or wood in the forests and pitched tents made of hide in the open. Today most Lapps are no longer nomadic. They work as foresters, fishermen, or on farms. Some even work in the mines.

Above: In Mongolia children learn to ride a horse as soon as (or before) they can walk. Keeping a watchful eye on the camels is more fun when you have a pony for a companion.

MIGRANT WORKERS

Some farm workers in developed countries move from place to place to find work. They move to an area as fruit or vegetable crops grow ripe. They pick them for low wages and live in temporary housing, often with poor sanitary facilities. These people generally live in poverty because their work is seasonal and low-paying, and they do not stay in one place long enough to receive the government benefits to which their poverty entitles them.

COMMUNES AND COLLECTIVES

In most countries farmers own their own land. Sons and daughters may help with work on the farm, and the same piece of land may stay in one family for hundreds of years. But sometimes the family sells the land to another farmer or to somebody who wants to build houses or factories on it. In some countries the land is taken from rich landowners by the government.

Collective farms

In the 1930s the communist government in Russia took land away from farmers and forced people to work on big state-run farms. This collective farming did not work very well because most people were happier tending their own small plots of land. Other communist countries tried similar plans, but most have had to return to a

COOPERATION AND
CORPORATE FARMS

Farmers often join together in voluntary cooperatives. Five dairy farmers in one area might get a better price for their milk if they sell it together. Grain farmers often band together to build an elevator where all their wheat can be stored and sold. People have more of an incentive to work hard on land of their own that they can pass on to a son or daughter, but often that is not the most efficient way to farm. Some family farms have evolved into large businesses and are run as corporate farms.

system that allows small farmers more freedom to spend their time working on their own land.

In China some farmhands also have jobs in factories. Women work in the fields by day and at night try to make more money by making clothes. Often grandparents, parents, and children live together in one farmhouse. They keep pigs, sheep, and cattle, and grow rice, vegetables, and herbs. Farmers in northern China grow wheat because the climate is too cold for rice. But in the warm south rice and other crops can be grown all year round.

A plot of one's own

A Chinese farm family lives simply. For many, home is a house made from mud bricks. Inside there may be a few modern conveniences now that electricity has reached most Chinese villages. People listen to the radio, and a

China has more people, and more farmers, than any other country. During the upheavals of the "Cultural Revolution" in the 1960s, many townspeople were moved to the country to work on communal farms (below left). In remote regions like Sinkiang Uighur, in northwest China, luxuries are in short supply. In this settlement (below, right) horseback riders outnumber trucks.

few lucky families own a television. Almost everyone rides a bicycle. Some people own motorbikes, but very few people can afford a car or truck. People walk miles along the dusty roads, carrying farm produce on their backs to sell in the market.

Some Chinese farmers still live in communes. These government-run farms are like small towns with their own schools, hospitals, and nurseries for babies. Everyone joins in the work in the communal fields, but each family also has a private plot and can choose which crops to grow and sell.

Life on a kibbutz

In Israel many farm families live on kibbutzim. These are communal farms, where people share everything. The kibbutz owns all property. The people make their own rules and vote on matters that affect the community. Everyone has a job. In return for their work, everyone receives food, shelter, education, and medical care. Young children spend their day in the nursery in the children's house while their parents are at work. They hardly see their parents during the day. But families meet to talk and relax in the communal dining room. Here the day starts early with breakfast together and ends with supper when the day's work is over.

Much of Israel is desert, land that is too dry to be farmed. The first kibbutz was set up in 1909. In 1948

Above: People on a kibbutz in Israel picking grapefruit. Working together is part of kibbutz life.

Left: A kibbutz community is like an extended family. The children learn, play, and eat as a group while their parents are working.

the modern state of Israel was founded. Thousands of Jews from Europe and elsewhere came to live there. They needed food. With the help of grants and loans from abroad, the people set about reclaiming the desert by skillful irrigation. They now grow numerous crops and export fruit and vegetables to countries all around the world.

The kibbutz settlements succeed because the people who live on them share a common purpose. People are ready to give up some privacy and individual freedom because they see benefits in working together. They live as pioneers in a new country, overcoming many dangers and difficulties.

THREAT OF WAR

The Israelis have made the desert green, but for many years their land has known no peace because of Israel's quarrel with its Arab neighbors. Many kibbutzim are within range of hostile forces. They have fortifications and are guarded night and day.

FARMING IN THE MODERN WORLD

Farmers often look back to the past when the farmer was a pioneer who cleared the land, tilled the virgin soil, and turned wilderness into fruitful fields. Farm life was at the heart of every nation. Farming in the future will be very different.

Natural disasters usually hit the poor hardest. Locusts are the scourge of African farmers. One swarm of these insects can destroy a year's crop in minutes.

In the past, almost all farms were family-sized and family-run. In poor countries most farms are still small. Governments and aid organizations encourage farmers to work together in communes. A peasant owning a tiny plot of land cannot produce food efficiently. A group of neighbors forming a commune can afford to buy better seeds, fertilizers, and farm tools. The commune can afford to hire a tractor and pay the vet to treat sick animals. Everyone benefits. The farmers decide together how the farm will be run and share the proceeds.

Green revolution

The world's farmers produce more food than ever before. Scientists have brought about a green revolution through the use of improved fertilizers and pesticides and advances in crop improvement and animal breeding. These advances have helped feed the world's hungry millions. Yet in famine-stricken countries, such as Ethiopia, people still die of starvation. The Earth's human population is growing at an alarming rate while the amount of land available for farming is unlikely to increase. Can we grow enough food to feed 10 billion people in the next century? No one can be sure.

Farming tomorrow

Today there are fewer farms and fewer farmers. In the 1930s there were more than six million farms in the

Drought and civil war have brought famine to parts of Africa. These hungry people in Ethiopia wait patiently for food brought by relief workers.

United States. Now there are only two million. In 1900 the average size of an American farm was 145 acres. Now it is three times as big: 455 acres. Many farms have become more like factories.

Farms today have fewer farm workers. In the 1800s one farm worker was needed to grow enough food for four people. Now, with modern methods, a single farm worker can produce enough food for 80 people.

From farms to factories

Some farming communities have gone forever. The Santa Clara Valley, near San Francisco in California, was once a rich orchard region, with farms producing plums, pears, apricots, cherries, and other fruits. The orchards have now gone, and in their place are computer factories. Orchard Valley has become Silicon Valley, a busy industrial and business region.

Changing tastes

The modern farmer must heed the demands of stores and customers. If shoppers want more chicken and less beef, then the beef farmer may find his income dwindling and may have to change to raising chickens.

GREEN WORLD

Only a few of the world's natural habitats remain. Most of the forests and grasslands have been turned into farmland. Overuse of the land and pollution from fertilizers and pesticides have created many environmental problems that must be solved before more damage is done. The world's tropical forests are now under threat. Many trees are being cut down for timber or burned to clear for farmland.

Forest communities in Asia and South America have tried to stop the destruction of the forests on which they depend. But they are powerless against the logging companies with their bulldozers and chain saws. If the world is to remain green and healthy, international measures must be taken to stop natural habitats from being destroyed.

Opposite: Once this land in Israel was desert. Now, thanks to soil irrigation and good soil management, olive trees thrive.

Above: Science can make barren soil bloom. Alaska has a harsh climate. But with modern seeds and techniques, barley can now be grown there. With improved varieties and better control of the environment, many more unproductive areas could be cultivated to feed the world's poor.

Farmers in less-developed countries who grow single crops such as cocoa or coffee are hard hit if prices drop because people eat less chocolate or decide that drinking too much coffee is bad for their health.

Some farmers have to sell their land to make room for housing, factories, or a new road. Where there is overproduction of a particular crop, governments encourage farmers to use their land in other ways. Some have made their farms into vacation homes, golf courses, or parks where townspeople can come to enjoy country life and see farm animals. The farmer may make more money from tourism than from farming.

Facing the challenge

In most countries the traditional picture-book farm, with its farmyard and mixture of animals, has vanished. The modern farmer is more likely to sit at a computer than to drive a horse and wagon. But farmers are still tied to their land. Their lives are governed by the rhythm of the seasons. Farmers everywhere face the same challenge. They must work in harmony with nature to produce our food but also work to protect the environment and the plants and animals that share our world.

Glossary

Auction Public sale in which crops, animals, or other articles are sold to the highest bidder.

Bartering Exchanging produce or goods for someone else's produce or goods.

Battery hens Hens reared and fattened in sheds for their eggs or meat.

Breed A particular kind of animal or plant. Farmers breed animals and plants by helping them produce offspring. They produce new varieties by breeding different types with different qualities.

Bunkhouses Simple buildings providing sleeping quarters for cowboys and other workers. With several beds to a room, the cowboys "bunked up" together.

Cash crops Crops grown for sale, not to be eaten by the farmer's family.

Cereal crops Food plants such as wheat, rice, barley, oats, millet, and sorghum.

Collective farms Formed from several small holdings. Voluntary collectives have produced efficient results in some countries, but state-controlled collectives in communist countries have usually been less successful.

Combine harvester Machine that cuts wheat (and other cereals) and separates the grain from the stalks, ready for storing.

Commune Community where people share everything and decide together how to run their affairs.

Cooperative An arrangement by which farmers run their own farms but work together to sell their produce.

Corporate farm Farm owned and operated by a large business or corporation. Some corporate farms are family farms.

Crop rotation Planting a different crop in a plot of land each season.

Rotation prevents the buildup of plant disease in the soil.

Dairy foods Foods such as butter, cheese, and yogurt that are made from milk.

Digging sticks Wooden implements used for turning the soil which farmers used before metal tools were invented. Digging sticks are still used in some countries.

Domesticate To make animals tame enough to rear and breed for food and other uses.

Drought Period without rainfall.

Elevator A grain elevator is a tall building, usually made of steel, that is used to store grain.

Factory farms On factory farms animals, such as calves or chickens, are not allowed to range freely. They are confined to and fed in temperature-controlled sheds.

Fallow land Farmland that is allowed to rest for a year or season without a crop to regain its fertility.

Famines When food supplies become extremely scarce and people starve to death. They may be caused by severe drought, crop failure, war, or overpopulation.

Fertilizer A natural or artificial chemical substance that is added to soil to make it more fertile.

Food processing Methods used to keep food from going bad and to present it in a form that pleases the customer.

Germinate A seed germinates when it puts down a root and sends up its first shoot. Seeds need water to germinate.

Gluts When the supply of a crop or product exceeds the demand for it.

Grain Seeds from wheat and other cereal plants that contain nutritious starch, protein, and oil.

Habitat Natural home of a plant or animal, or a collection of them.

Harvest Time for, or the act of gathering, ripe crops.

Herbicides Chemicals used to kill plants. Most are selective, killing weeds while leaving crops undamaged.

Intensive farming Methods used to get as high a yield as possible from farmland or farm animals.

Irrigation Watering crops by artificial means, for example, by digging canals and ditches to carry water from a river.

Kibbutzim Farm communities in Israel, where people live and work together, sharing everything.

Latex Liquid that oozes from a rubber tree and is used to make rubber.

Legumes Members of the pea family. They produce their seeds in pods, and their roots fix nitrogen in the soil and make it more fertile.

Livestock Animals that are raised on farms for use or sale.

Longhouses Communal houses in which many families share accommodations.

Market Place where goods are bought and sold. Farmers in many countries carry their own produce or drive their animals to market in the nearest town.

Mechanize To use machines to do jobs that were formerly done by people.

Mixed farm A farm where crops are grown and animals are reared. An arable farm grows only crops. Other farms such as pig farms, ranches, or sheep stations keep only animals.

Monsoon Wind that brings the wet and dry seasons to south and east Asia.

Nomads   People who move their homes constantly with their herds of grazing animals, such as sheep, cattle, or camels.

Orchard   Plantation of fruit trees, such as apples, pears, or plums.

Peasant   A farmer who owns a small plot of land.

Perishable   Foods that do not keep for long and have to be preserved in some way.

Pesticides   Chemicals used to kill insect pests.

Pharaoh   King in ancient Egypt.

Pioneers   Original settlers who make the way ready for others.

Plantations   Large farms planted with a single crop, such as cotton, tea, or bananas.

Plow   A farm tool used for turning the soil to ready it for planting. Also, the act of using a plow.

Pollution   The dirtying of the environment with poisonous or unpleasant substances.

Portage   The act of transporting or carrying.

Prairies   Flat or rolling treeless plains that were naturally grass-covered and are now used for growing wheat.

Produce   Food or other products from a farm or plantation.

Ranches   Very large farms where cattle or other animals are reared. In Australia they are called stations.

Range   Large, open stretch of grazing land.

Reclaiming   Bringing land back into use that was formerly unusable, such as desert or land that was flooded.

Retailers   Merchants who sell goods in small quantities to the public. Wholesalers sell in larger quantities to retailers. Producers, such as farmers, sell in bulk to wholesalers.

Rustlers   Cattle thieves, so-called because a rustle may be the loudest sound they make as they spirit away the cattle.

Scythes   Tools with long curved blades and long wooden handles used by farmers to cut crops.

Seasons   Times of the year with distinct climates. In temperate regions, the four seasons are winter, spring, summer, and autumn (fall).

Serfs   People who worked on the land and were partly slaves. Serfdom was widespread during the Middle Ages and persisted in Russia until this century.

Settlers   People who move to live in a new area. America is peopled by the descendants of settlers from all over the world.

Shadoof   Device used for irrigating fields in ancient Egypt. It consists of a bucket on the end of a long pole and can be powered by people or tethered animals.

Shearing   Cutting away the wool, or fleece, of sheep.

Sickles   Tools with short handles and semicircular blades used by farmers to cut crops.

Stampedes   Sudden scatterings of cattle or other animals panicking in fright.

Steppes   European equivalent of the prairies.

Subsistence farmers   Farmers who grow just enough to feed one family, or village, with nothing left over for sale.

Temperate zones   Zones with a moderate climate with four seasons. They lie between the tropics and the polar regions.

Tenants   People who have temporary ownership of land or dwellings.

Tepees   Conical tents made of skins stretched over a frame of converging poles.

Terraced hillsides   Hills with a series of level areas cut into them, like steps. They retain enough soil and moisture for farmers to grow crops that could never grow on the natural slopes.

Third World   Term used to describe the poor and under-developed nations of the world. Most Third World countries are in Africa and Asia.

Tied cottages   In Britain homes for farmhands that go with the job. If the farmhand loses his job, he loses his home, too.

Wholesalers   Merchants who buy goods and produce from producers to sell to retailers.

Wigwams   Indian shelters.

Yield   The amount of a crop or crops that a piece of land produces.

Index